Window in Time:
The Story of the Discovery of the Casper Site

By
Roderick D. Laird
Illustrations by
John T. Gilman

A Book of Western History and Prehistory

A Window in Time;

The Story of the Discovery of the Casper Site.
© Copyright 1992, Roderick D. Laird.
All rights reserved.

On the cover, clockwise from the top left;
diorama of a buffalo kill site, a buffalo skull
uncovered at the Casper Site, uncovering the bones,
a Clovis point from the site, a Hell Gap point from the site,
a spearpoint mounted on an Atlatl shaft.

Cover photographs and photographs on pages 33 - 35
by Jennifer Laird, Pat Laird and the author.

Saratoga Museum Papers
Number 2   July 1992

ISBN 0-936204-46-X

Jelm Mountain Press – 1992 – Laramie, Wyoming

Special thanks to :
Reader's Digest,
National Endowment for the Humanities,
Lynne V. Cheney, Chairman
- and -
Saratoga Historical and Cultural Association
Saratoga, Wyoming
"The Birthplace of Modern Atlatl Competition"

For Pat

The Discovery

Casper, Wyoming. Sunday, March 28, 1971 . . .

In frontier journals there are accounts of homestead wives who, driven mad by the incessant wind, would crack and run screaming from their lonely soddies into the emptiness of the plains. It was that kind of day, not unusual for that time of year in Wyoming. The chinook gusting across the treetops in the big tree district of the city would be moving freely across the plains and the sand hills north and east of town. In hundreds of blowouts, countless tiny grains of quartz would be bouncing along the surface, moving relentlessly south-west to northeast. Ripples, like slow motion waves on a lake, would be moving forward as the scouring action of the wind dug down ever deeper . . . *through old surfaces and soils, down through ancient pond deposits . . . down, down into the distant past when Ice Age hunters roamed the land. Stone tools and weapon points, lost in the confusion of the hunt so long ago, would be uncovered this day, here and there in the vast expanse of sand hills . . . wherever a moving dune exposed an ancient camp or kill site.*

The thought was just too much for my good friend Dave, and me, as we discussed the possibilities for the day. The long winter had brought out a bad case of cabin fever, and we felt a driving need to get out and pursue our favorite hobby: searching for signs of ancient people. In our minds the prospect of finding ancient artifacts easily outweighed the discomfort of the biting wind. We had to go look! Now, could we persuade the ladies?

Jamie, Dave's wife, preferred the idea of catching some late-season skiing at Hogadon. Pat Davies, my fiancee, was spending the weekend in her sister's home; she would have to begin the long drive back to Colorado Springs that afternoon, fighting the gusty crosswinds. On the telephone she was reluctant at first . . . . *Dave and I pleaded our case . . . . Fortunately for American archaeology, they both finally agreed to humor us.* Minutes later we were headed for the sand hills north of the city.

We would go to my favorite spot — a large moving dune which trailed twin ridges behind it, tracing its movement over the past several thousand years. Each winter it marched forward as much as twelve feet, and as it moved across the ancient hunting grounds it uncovered bones and artifacts from long ago. It would be our best bet!

Dave Egolf had grown up in Casper and his curiosity about ancient times had begun in childhood. On Dead Horse Hill near his home he had found fossils which had kindled his interest in the past, and an occasional Indian artifact found on outings with his father, a geologist, had fired his imagination even more.

My involvement in amateur archaeology had also begun in my youth, in Cheyenne County, Kansas, and Prowers County, Colorado, where old-timers told tales of Dust Bowl days when ancient campsites and countless

1
For awhile it appeared we would beat the storm.

artifacts had been uncovered near the shorelines of lakes long disappeared. Large areas of the vast High Plains had been stripped of the vital shortgrass cover by the plow of the wheat farmer, and the priceless topsoil had blown away, often to surprising depths, revealing the deeply buried clues to the past. But the interest of my youth had turned into a passion during my college days when I found ancient artifacts myself in the San Luis Valley of Colorado, and in the country around Gallup, New Mexico, where I landed my first teaching job . . . . And then, while in graduate school at Eastern New Mexico University, I was drafted to do salvage work at the world-famous Blackwater Draw. We were racing the earth-moving equipment at Sam Sanders' gravel pit to try to save Clovis and Folsom material from destruction. There I had learned to recognize the bones of the long-extinct megafauna of the Pleistocene such as the mammoth and the longhorn bison, and there my interest matured from that of an artifact hunter to the level of a serious student of the intriguing scientific realm which lies beyond the superficial collecting of artifacts.

I began to wonder, *"Who were these people who made such beautiful weapon points? What were they like? How was the environment different then?"*

Upon leaving ENMU in 1964 and moving to Casper, I expressed my regrets to Dr. George Agogino about leaving the rich archaeology of New Mexico. However, he was

2
The four of us walked across the rippled surface . . . . It did not look promising . . . .

confident I would find an ancient-man site in Wyoming if I would just get out and search for one.

And now, some seven years later, I had no idea that his prophecy was about to come true . . . .

As we neared our target dune we kept an uneasy eye on an ominous black storm front approaching from the north. For awhile it appeared that we would beat the storm, but as we came into sight of our goal, the front stampeded past us and the dune disappeared from view, obscured by thick, swirling goosedown snowflakes riding a north wind. Within seconds the prairie around us was covered with a cold, white blanket of snow. Reluctantly, we turned around and groped our way back to the interstate. The day was a total loss! No one spoke much on the long ride back to town. Halfway there, we broke out of the storm, and as we approached Casper it appeared we might salvage a short hunt somewhere near the city. I had been watching an area of blowing sand by the new Control Data plant for several weeks. A stabilized sand hill had been partly removed by earth-moving equipment and the wind had been working on the bare field of sand where the hill had been. I had never stopped there to look — after all, it was right beside the highway! But, this time, driven back by the sudden spring storm, we couldn't be too choosy, and in the back of my mind was the lesson learned from Bob Howard, another one of my hunting buddies: he had found some of

3
"It can't be . . ."

JOHN T. GILMAN 1990

his best artifacts right beside roads, looking in places so obvious that others had overlooked them.

As we passed the blowing field of sand right by the city limits sign, I impulsively suggested, "Hey, let's look there for a few minutes!"

The four of us walked across the rippled surface of the newly-formed blowout, which was rapidly deflating. Until recently, this had been buried about thirty feet deep; in constructing the Control Data factory the earthmovers had taken the southern two-thirds of a sand hill and had spread it to the south to fill in the location for the building and its parking lot. Not long before our arrival a jogger had run right through the center of the sandy area, which was about the size of two football fields, for his tracks and those of his two dogs had not yet been erased by the wind.

The site did not look at all promising and after a few minutes we were ready to give it up. The wind had too much of an edge; our eyes were watering from the icy blast and the stinging grains of sand, which were reaching altitudes of six feet and more. There appeared to be no sign of early man in the shifting sand — no camp rocks, no chips, no bones . . . *but suddenly, a mind-jarring shape caught my attention!*

About thirty feet ahead of me the rear fins of a Clovis point were protruding from the slope of one of the ripples! I knew at once what it was, even from that distance, but

4
The others came rushing over . . .

JOHN T. GILMAN 1990

some doubting part of my mind refused to believe the message arriving through my eyes.

"Oh, no!" I heard a shaking voice say, "It can't be!" The voice was mine . . . .

I rushed over and knelt down. With trembling fingers I brushed sand away from the covered portion of the beautiful moss agate projectile point. It was . . . *complete! And unmistakably Clovis, a culture dating back approximately 11,200 years! Leaping to my feet, I began to jump and dance in a frenzy of joy as the doubting corner of my brain grudgingly admitted the magnitude of the discovery. Prying the new gray Stetson from my head (it had been screwed down tight to ear level to keep it from blowing into Nebraska) I pitched it high up into the gale and began to yell incoherently!*

The others came rushing over to see what was causing such a celebration. Pat chased down my hat on her way toward me. When Dave got within a few yards of me he stopped abruptly, his unbelieving stare riveted to another dark shape in the moving sand. Then he began to whoop and dance. Quickly we gathered around. It was another Ice Age projectile point — this time a Hell Gap, broken but still recognizable as a 10,000 year old spear-point named after its discovery location: Hell Gap, Wyoming, near Guernsey.

Two Paleoindian points in one spot — *this* spot! It seemed incredible! Physical discomfort quickly was forgotten as we eagerly scoured the area around our

5
It was another
Paleoindian point!

JOHN T. GILMAN 1990

finds. We were seeing bone slivers now, and bright white fragments of tooth enamel. Then I picked up a complete tooth — a giant molar . . . *a bison molar, but not from a modern bison. It was so large that it had to be from one of the ancient longhorned bison of the Pleistocene!*

The search produced no more artifacts, but we considered ourselves lucky indeed, and left . . . *still unaware of the archaeological treasure which was resting only a few inches under our feet.*

Back at the Egolf's house, we laid the 10,000 year-old point beside the older one on the dining room table. Against the contrast of the white tablecloth, their beauty of design and craftsmanship was striking. The Clovis was made of a spectacular brown and clear chalcedony which looked very similar to a Montana moss agate, or a Sweetwater agate. The Hell Gap was flaked from a fine-grained quartzite, probably from the "Spanish Diggings" area. Gazing in awe at these ancient artifacts, which were utilitarian and yet art forms as well, was a mystic experience. I have since learned that there is a considerable amount of evidence that these points were an important aspect of the hunters' religious beliefs — perhaps we were picking up some of the thoughts and feelings that went into the making of the points, and the accompanying ceremonies . . . *or perhaps we were just moved by the beauty of the artistic expression. At any rate, it had been quite a day . . . .*

6
Just as we got to our goal, another blizzard struck. The prairie was covered almost immediately.

JOHN T. GILMAN 1989

13

Casper. Saturday, April 3, 1971 . . .

The next weekend Pat again came to Casper, and the four of us decided to try again to reach the distant dune which had been our goal before. This time, because of the excitement generated by our finds, there was no debate on what we should do; destiny was calling! We crammed ourselves into my El Camino and headed out the interstate.

It was on this day that Dave and I began to be aware of some of the coincidences of this story. A hard-to-define feeling started to arc back and forth between us. When it was all over we would swear that the Ancient Ones had been speaking to us!

What could have passed for the very same dark cloud bank of the week before was hanging on the northern horizon. The same kind of race took place, and the same kind of tie. Just as we got to our goal another spring blizzard struck. The prairie was covered with wet, sticky snow almost immediately. This time we had actually piled out of the car and had started climbing the steep flank of the dune before we were stopped by the snow.

At that moment, rather than feeling frustrated as we had the week before, Dave and I looked at each other as if suddenly comprehending an obvious truth, and simultaneously exclaimed, "I think they want us to go back and look there again!"

"They" who? And why had the same thought occurred to us both, at the same instant?

7
By noon we knew for certain . . .
We were looking through a window in time.

Within an hour we had broken out of the storm, again, and we were back at the blowing field of sand by Control Data. We found no more artifacts, but more bone evidence had been uncovered. Two areas of bone fragments and teeth seemed to be remnants of skulls which had been exposed during the week of ceaseless wind and, having dried out, had disintegrated. Small fragments of bone were blowing away even as we watched. Several ribs and other bones had also been exposed.

Still not realizing that we had discovered a major site, we headed back to the El Camino. Jamie, Pat and I piled in, but Dave grabbed a shovel and went back into the stinging gale. He began to dig carefully, near one of the bone fragment concentrations. Almost at once, he waved frantically for us to come back! He had dug into a section of articulated vertebrae of a large animal! The loose sand was quite easy to dig and it brushed away from the bones without effort. We sank test holes in half a dozen places. Everywhere we struck bone, and only a few inches from the surface! It began to dawn on us at last that we had been walking over something of major importance, but a question still remained. Could the bones be related to one of the points we'd found that first day?

The bones were in excellent condition and it was hard to believe that they could be as old as either of the points we had found on the surface. Yet, many of the bones

8
The site was right by the interstate.

showed unmistakable butchering marks — scars left by stone tools.

We decided to meet at the site the next morning and try to find out if we actually had, as we now suspected, found a bison kill of extreme antiquity.

* * * *

The Casper Site. Sunday, April 4, 1971 . . .

The four of us worked intently all morning with trowels, paintbrushes, and our fingers, hardly noticing the cold or the stinging sand grains. We were all feeling crackling sparks of excitement as we very carefully uncovered bone after bone, appearing to be much too well-preserved to be old, yet all too large to be modern. After short breaks in the Camino with hot coffee and rolls and excited conversation, we'd get back to our task. Some of the vertebrae showed remains of tall dorsal spines, the supports for a bison's hump — and all had been hacked off to remove the choice cut of meat!

By noon we knew for certain what we had. Three bison skulls had been uncovered, and each showed the distinctive wide hornspan that obviously belonged to no bison of today. We were looking through a window in time! These were the remains of animals thousands of years old and now extinct! And the butchering marks told us the bison had met their Waterloo at the hands of ancient hunters . . . .

9
Dr. Frison and a crew from the University of Wyoming excavated the site.

JOHN T. GILMAN 1990

We held a brief conference in the Camino to decide what to do. Then we set to work, carefully covering up with sand what we had brushed clear, and leaving the bones and skulls undisturbed. We removed one mandible in order to demonstrate the identity of the species. Within minutes the blowing sands dried out the moisture and erased the signs of our digging; the ripples began to form again.

We raced to a telephone to call the state archaeologist. There was no doubt about it now; we had made a discovery of major significance, and we had to make sure the scientists got to it before the vandals!

State Archaeologist George Frison had been addressing the Wyoming Archaeological Society at the Holiday Inn, hardly more than a stone's throw from where we had been digging, while we were digging . . . His topic? *"Early Man's Bison Butchering Techniques."* By the time he returned to his home in Laramie, his phone was ringing . . . .

Understandably enough, Dr. Frison was reluctant to get back in the saddle and return to Casper on the say-so of four excited amateurs. He told us to have John Albanese, a Casper geologist, look at the evidence. We rushed to the home of Albanese and showed him the points and mandible. John thought, as we had at first, that the bone was too well-preserved to be very old — he suggested that the bone bed might mark a spot where "a herd of longhorn cattle had been caught in a blizzard in the late

1800's." But the Clovis point was too significant to disregard; in the end, the Clovis would persuade Frison to come have a look.

Thus, our discovery entered the scientific record of the peopling of the Americas. Within two months Dr. Frison and a crew from the University of Wyoming would spend a month excavating much of the site, which proved to be Hell Gap.

In the summer of 1974, the crew returned to dig the rest of the site. During this second excavation, evidence was unearthed which may explain the presence of the Clovis point: bones from a camel were found. This creature, present in Clovis times but thought to have been extinct by the time of the Hell Gap hunters, very well might have been brought down by Clovis hunters. That evidence then, would have been present at the site for 1,000 years before the Hell Gap hunters slaughtered a bison herd on the same spot.

The dozens of Hell Gap points found among the bison bones by the scientists, and the tools and the bones themselves, revealed the story of what had happened at the site, and when, leaving only the details not filled in.

That story, including generous helpings of inference and speculation (but based upon evidence from Hell Gap sites), follows:

The Hunt

A sand dune above the Great River by the Black Mountains. Fall, 10,000 Years B.P . . . .

Slowly, silently, the shaman eased into position downwind from the herd of longhorn bison. Other members of the gathered clans, all experienced in the ways of their bison brothers and sisters, had slowly maneuvered the herd into position off to the side of the trail they usually used in moving from their watering place back to the nutritious grasses of the rolling plains north of the river.

Kneeling behind a clump of yucca, the shaman surveyed the scene. The hunters and drivers were all in position, watching his hiding place for the signal. Forty summers in age, the shaman was an old man for his time and place and was revered by his people for his wisdom and experience. He checked his miniature magic spear, a replica of the ones carried by the hunters surrounding the dune-trap — the same but for the fact that it was only sixteen inches long and tipped with a tiny stone point of the same design as the hunters' full-sized ones. His miniature spearpoint was smeared with the same magic paint made from ground red ochre which covered the full-sized tips of the hunters' weapons. The red coating, applied during a solemn ceremony the night before, would provide the spears with life of their own and ensure that they would fly true to their marks. The symbolic blood

10
Drivers popped up at precisely the right moments.

JOHN T. GILMAN 1991

ritual had never been known to fail, except, of course, when the ceremony had not been performed properly. It was the shaman's responsibility to see that the necessary rituals were performed properly . . . and also to lure the shaggy brothers and sisters into the trap. If he were to fail, the clans would go hungry during the months of snow, which now were not far off. *Gently, he smoothed the delicate fletching on the little spear and then tied it with a string of soft buckskin to the little atlatl, also a miniature copy of the weapons carried by the hunters. His right hand went to the medicine bag at his throat, then passed over the model atlatl and spear in his left hand. He muttered the magic words, asking permission of the bison brothers and sisters to take their lives. He pulled the bison robe over his head and stood up.*

At the sight of the shaman standing, the signal they had been waiting for, the drivers tensed, beginning their countdown. They watched as the shaman began the bison dance, luring the herd further from their trail and toward the dune-trap. Curious, the boss cow, leader of the herd, began to move toward the shaman. Others in the herd raised their heads from their nervous feeding, moving after the lead cow . . . .

The drivers jumped up in sequence, whooping loudly and waving skins. Panicked, the rearmost bison wheeled and stampeded toward the dune, pushing those in front of them. The shaman, still holding the miniature weapons in one hand and clutching the bison robe in the other,

11
The hunters fired at the bison with their atlatls.

began to sprint for the dune — the lead cow racing after him, followed by the thundering herd. Additional drivers popped up at precisely the right moments to turn the herd at just the right angle, to make sure they stampeded into the steep-sided bowl of the blowout.

The operation went without a hitch; the shaman sprinted across the hardpan floor of the blowout and on up the leeward slope. The bison, unable to navigate in the soft sand of the sides of the dune, began to slow and mill around on the floor of the bowl as the hunters appeared above the steep sides and all along the leeward slope, firing at the bison with their atlatls. Red-smeared stone tips flashed in the crisp autumn air as the five-foot long darts, fletched with turkey wing feathers, spun toward their targets.

Many hundreds of spears were cast; over a hundred animals were downed. Only a few escaped, running back toward the river, the way they had entered the trap. The hunt was a success. Once again the rituals had worked. There would be feasting on hump and liver and tongue, and there would be jerky aplenty for all the clans during the coming winter.

The women and children moved in to begin the immense job of skinning and butchering, using razor-sharp stone knives and tools manufactured on the spot from bison bones. The hunters feasted on raw liver as they searched the killing ground looking for any spears, foreshafts, or points that could be salvaged. They

12
The women and children began the skinning and butchering.

JOHN I GILMAN 1991

27

would recycle broken points and rebuild the precious spear shafts whenever possible. Soon, a steady stream of meat was being packed out of the sand to the drying platforms in the camp outside the dune.

The celebration and ceremony thanking the brothers and sisters would last well into the night, and the story of the hunt would be told and retold by all the far-flung clans long after they split up for the long winter. Indeed, this kill would be recalled for many generations, passed along in the oral tradition of the clans of The People.

When the tens of thousands of pounds of meat had been converted to the much lighter and more compact jerky, The People began to separate, each clan going its own direction, and taking with them their share of the robes, jerky, and other products of the kill.

Even before The People had left their camp beside the dune, the moving sand had begun to drift over the remains of the bison. Within a few days, all traces of the kill were completely covered. Not many years later, following a period of slightly increased rainfall, a pond formed in the bottom of the blowout. Sediment sinking to the bottom of the pond sealed the sand deposits with a layer of mud. The pond disappeared during an ensuing dry cycle, and the mud turned into a hardpan armor which sealed and protected the evidence of the hunt. Eventually a thirty-foot sand ridge was deposited over the spot, and for 10,000 years the archaeological treasure remained undisturbed . . . .

13
Not many years later,
a pond formed
in the blowout.

Epilogue

Miraculously, much of the site survived construction of a pipeline through one side of the bone deposit, and the earth-moving project which leveled the protective sand hill during construction of the Control Data plant and parking lot. I learned in an interview with the foreman that the pipeline crew noticed bones and artifacts, and picked up some which their machines had tossed into the backdirt. No one reported the find. The heavy-equipment operators leveling the sand hill also must have noticed some of the site material. Luckily, their machines stopped inches above most of the bone layer. Only a small area of the deposit was destroyed.

A present day dune north of the Platte River. The Casper Site hunters used a similar feature for their bison trap.

The jogger, with his two dogs, must have run past the two points without noticing them. We came along at just the right moment, looking for just such a discovery. Even so, it took two tries before the message soaked in . . . .

A few odds and ends: I still have the gray Stetson, though now it bears little resemblance to the nifty hat I tossed into the air that day. During the winter of 1971-72 I took a friend out to the site, which had been covered back up, and we discovered that the relentless wind had deflated several feet of sand which had been used to cover the site. Bone material was again exposed in the unexcavated areas of the site. While walking across the blowout I found two broken Hell Gap points which had just been uncovered. These matched broken halves from the dig. One of these points is pictured on the cover of this

A pond has formed in this blowout, just as had happened at the Casper Site.

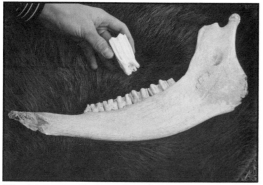

The bison tooth found on the surface, and the first mandible uncovered by the discovers.

Profile trench showing pond sediment (dark layer) that sealed the site for 10,000 years.
Photo courtesy of UW Anthropology Department.

A Hell Gap Point from the Casper Site.

Photographs by Jennifer Laird, Pat Laird, the author and courtesy of the University of Wyoming Anthropology Department.

Scott Laird demonstrating proper form in the use of the Atlatl.

Discoverers of the Casper Site: Rod Laird, Pat Laird, Jamie Egolf, and Dave Egolf at the site in 1972.

A Hell Gap point in-situ near a bison rib.
Photo courtesy of UW Anthropology Department.

book (lower left). To the right of it is the Clovis point which led to the discovery of the site. The scientific information gained from the dig was published in a book: *The Casper Site* by Dr. George Frison.

Though Dave and I had long hoped to find a paleo site that would be named after us, the state archaeologist declined our request. A few years later, another Hell Gap site was found on a ranch near Laird, Colorado, and I thought for sure there would be at least a Laird Site in the literature! But no such luck: the site director named that one the Jones-Miller Site, after the discoverers. Oh, well!

For me, our discovery was one of the great thrills of a lifetime — the kind which comes very rarely, if ever. It would be nineteen more years before such an experience, and such a thrill of discovery, would happen to me again. On the High Plains of Northwest Kansas I would notice an ancient spearpoint lying in a concentration of bison bone fragments. I would kneel in wonder and disbelief, hardly daring to reach out and touch that brown jasper message from the past . . . . *But, that's another story!*

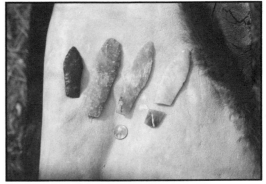

Hell Gap Points from the Casper Site.

Hell Gap Points from the Casper Site. The "stubby" ones were broken in use, and "recycled."